Forex Secret Trading Model

(Tools, Timing, and Forecasting)

Rich Finegan

Disclamer:

Foreign exchange trading carries a high level of risk and may not be suitable for you, please carefully consider your risk appetite and do not invest money that you cannot afford to lose

ISBN:1500542962
ISBN-13:9781500542962

DEDICATION:

To those who are serious in forex trading

CONTENTS

Preface

When you open forex charts, there are plenty of technical analysis tools available such as MACD, Stochastic, RSI, DMI, etc. what should we do about them? Are you going to use them all? Which one is the best? What is the best combination among them?

Business and forex trading are quite similar, they are having products to trade, and the product of forex trading is currency. In real business, we seldom see people use technical analysis tools such as MACD, RSI, Stochastic, DMI, etc. to buy or sell products, so why should we use those technical analysis tools as main tools to buy or sell currency? All technical analysis tools are just supporting tools for analysis; they should not be used as main tools for buying or selling decision. The market trend and market price is the real main tools to make buying or selling decision.

In this book we are combining: market price, trend line (to see the market trend), and technical analysis tool to form a powerful forex trading model. Trend line strategy itself is a powerful trading model, however when we combine it with technical analysis tool, there are more opportunities to explore.

Understanding this trading model may guide you become a pro forex analyst or trader and not just a person who read or hear "Buy" or "Sell" recommendation but also know the information when to execute it and know the reason behind the recommendation.

Good luck!

CHAPTER 1

BUSINESS AND FOREX TRADING ARE SIMILAR

How business works:

Imagine you are opening a flower store, before you buy flowers for inventory, you may want to know what kind of flowers are in demand now If today near valentine's day, maybe you should buy roses because the market demand/trend are roses, if today is December, Christmas flowers should be the inventory. These activities mean you are following market trend. If in early January some flowers stores start giving Christmas flower discount, even below their average buying prices, you should question this, why are they doing this? Ah... there are not many Christmas flower demand in January, the trend has changed, what you should do? You need to sell your Christmas flowers at discount to avoid loses.

How Forex trading works:

In forex trading, your inventory is currency, and before trading you may want to know what the currency trend is now, is it up trend or down trend. You may also ask some banks, brokers or friends to find out the answer. If majority mention up trend, you will make buying decision, on the other hand, you will make selling decision if majority mention down trend. This activities means you are following market trend.

If next week the currency price start going to the opposite ways from your current position, even below your average buying prices, you should question this, why are they doing this? Ah.... the country is cutting interest rate, the currency trend has changed, what you should do? You need to do a "cut loss" action to avoid further losses.

Both business and forex trading are quite similar, they are having something to trade, they need to know the market trend and they need to monitor market price to win the competition.

What we can conclude here, to win the market competition, we need to know two main information:

1. Market trend
2. Market price

CHAPTER 2

FOREX SECRET EXECUTION TOOLS

In business, market trend and market price information sometimes not available, knowing this information will differentiate the winner and loser.

In forex trading, market trend and market price information are available in the market. But why there are still losers if the information is available? Execution time and different tools used by market players cause this. There are many time frames of forex trading (5 minutes, 10 minutes, 1 hour, 8 hours, 1 day, 1 week, 1 month, etc) and also hundreds of technical analysis tools (many kinds of MACD, many kinds of Stochastic, RSI, momentum, etc. Including their different parameters) to interpret the data and create different strategy.

All technical analysis tools are using the same source of data which is price information, so price information should be the first confirmation for execution, not technical analysis tools.

From the prices we will know the market trend and also the market average price.

The secret execution tools:

1. Market Trend

As explained before, winner in business is about reading market trend to set up strategy. Market trend has been explained in detail in my previous book *"Forex Trend Line Trading Strategy, it is hard to win without knowing the trend"*. We are using non standard Parabolic SAR (Stop and Reverse) with parameter (0.02,0) to get the longer view of trends. The trend line is similar to a road structure which enables you to know your position and where is the next potential stop. The trend line will become the price support and resistance line.

Here are the steps to set up trend line:

    a. Determine two latest up and down trend in SAR group

    b. Determine the highest and lowest price among the two uptrend and down trend SAR group

    c. Draw lines among the highest and lowest price from those SAR group

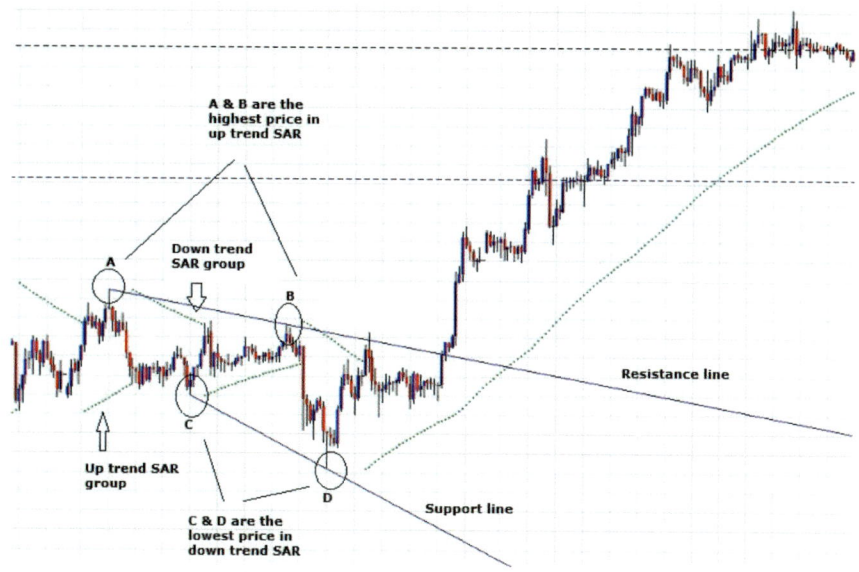

Chart 1 – Drawing trend line

A and B are the highest price between the 2 uptrend SAR group and we can draw a line to connect A and B to become a resistance line for future up trend price movement

C and D are the lowest price between the 2 down trend SAR group and we can draw line to connect C and D to become a support line for future down trend price movement.

2. Market Price

There are buying and selling activities to form market prices, for buyer it becomes buying cost and for seller it becomes selling price. To monitor market price activities during a period we need to see historical prices and find out what is the average price. To analyze and calculate market average price within a period we will use:

a. Simple Moving Average (SMA) or Moving Average (MA)

Moving average is a simple price average calculation by adding all the data and divided by number of data, for example: $(1+2+3+4+5)/5 = 3$.

We are using moving average 20, which represent 20 hourly data if you are using hourly time frame or 20 days data if you are using daily data. Why 20? If 1 day 24 hours and 1 month 24 trading days, by using 20 period we are 4 period ahead (faster 4 period) in identifying price activities.

b. Exponential Moving Average (EMA)

Exponential moving average give **faster price movement** as it reduces lags by applying more weight to recent prices. The weighting applied to the most recent price depends on the number of periods in the moving average. To analyze the market price, we are using EMA 20. Here is the formula to calculate EMA.

Period: 20

Multiplier= $2/(\text{time period}+1) = 2/(20+1) = 9,5\%$

EMA = (close price-EMA previous day) x multiplier + EMA previous day

Both SMA and EMA are available in most forex chart system.

Chart 2: EMA 20 and SMA 20 line

From chart 2, it shows that EMA 20 moves faster than SMA 20 to follow the latest price movement.

EMA and SMA concept seems simple and familiar by some traders but may not be their main focus as there are many technical analysis tools overrides this basic business concept.

3. Supporting technical analysis tools: Relative Strength Index (RSI)

Once we are familiar with trend line, moving average concept, we need a supporting technical analysis tool as second opinion to confirm the execution.

The parameter for RSI is 14 or RSI 14. RSI was introduced by Welles

Wilder in his book *New Concept in Technical Trading Systems*. Mr. Wilder also recommended using RSI 14. RSI is a price-following oscillator that ranges between 0 and 100, the buying strength is coming when RSI index shows 50 or above, RSI index below 50 means the selling strength is still there. We are not discussing RSI formula here as it is available in most forex chart systems, however if you want to know the detail, you can refer to Mr. Wilder's book.

Chart 3: RSI index line

By combining 2 main tools, trend line and moving Average plus Relative Strength Index (RSI), we can set buying and selling strategy and even forecast the potential price target.

CHAPTER 3

SECRET TRADING STRATEGY

There is trading strategy for trend line as discussed in my book "*Forex Trend Line Trading Strategy, it is hard to win without knowing the trend*" and there is no change for that strategy in this book, however we will combine trend line, moving average and RSI to maximize the opportunities or to act faster when the market against us. We are using one hour time frame in this book.

First Strategy:
Price close 2 times in a row above/below trend line (breaks support/resistance line)

In chart 4, there is buying signal when the price closes 2 times in a row above the trend line (resistance line). The most important thing is: drawing the correct trend line by using non standard Parabolic SAR (0.02,0). This strategy seems like taking advantage from the winner of bulls and bears price fighting within the trend line (support and resistance line). We let them fight within the trend line and we will follow the winner who breaks the trend line.

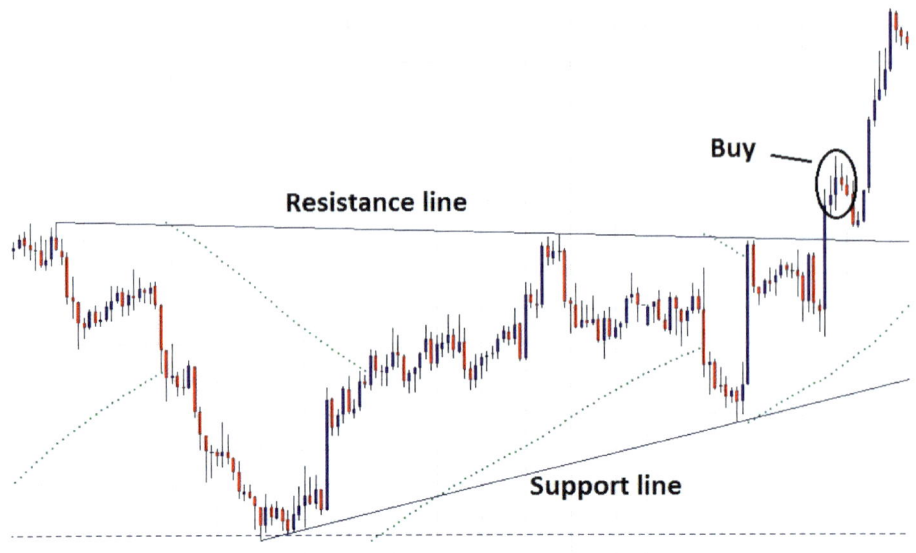

Chart 4: Trend line strategy

Although it is powerful, this strategy may take longer time to see the buying/selling signal as we do not know how long it takes to confirm the winner (break out).

Some traders may not be interested in this strategy as it is too slow and there are many opportunities in between support and resistance line. That is fine, if we do not want to wait for the winner, let's help them fights and go inside the market and fight in between resistance and support line. Here we come with the second strategy.

Second Strategy:

a. **BUYING SIGNAL**: EMA 20 line above SMA 20 line and price close above EMA 20 plus RSI 14 index at 50 or above.

Chart 5: Buying signal

b. **SELLING SIGNAL:** EMA 20 line below SMA 20 and price close below EMA 20 plus RIS 14 index below 50

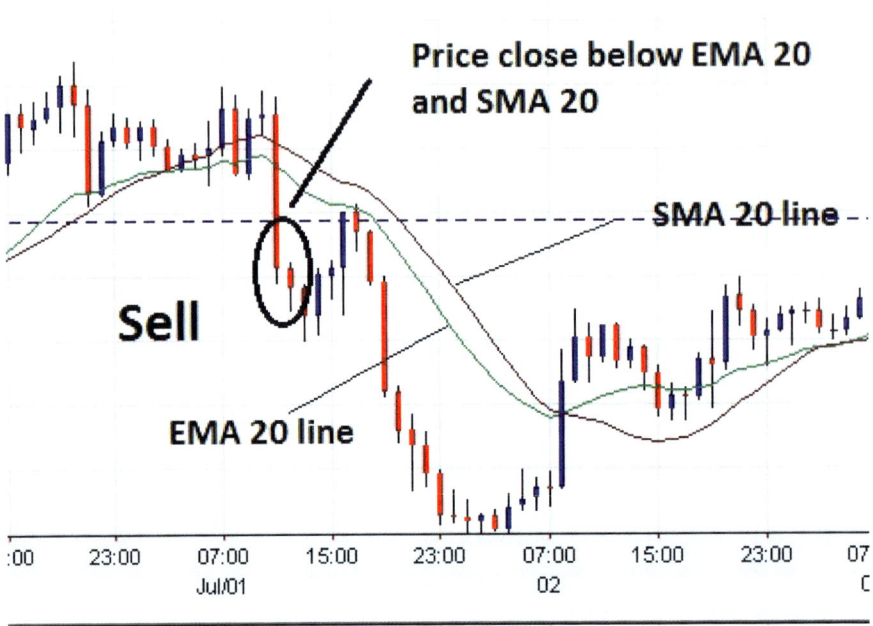

Chart 6: Selling signal

General rule: when price close above EMA 20 and SMA 20, RSI 14 will be at index 50 or above; when price close below EMA 20 and SMA 20, RSI 14 will be below index 50. If this condition is not satisfied, wait for the next hour for the confirmation.

Chart 7 shows false buying signals when price close above EMA 20 and SMA 20 but RSI 14 still below index 50.

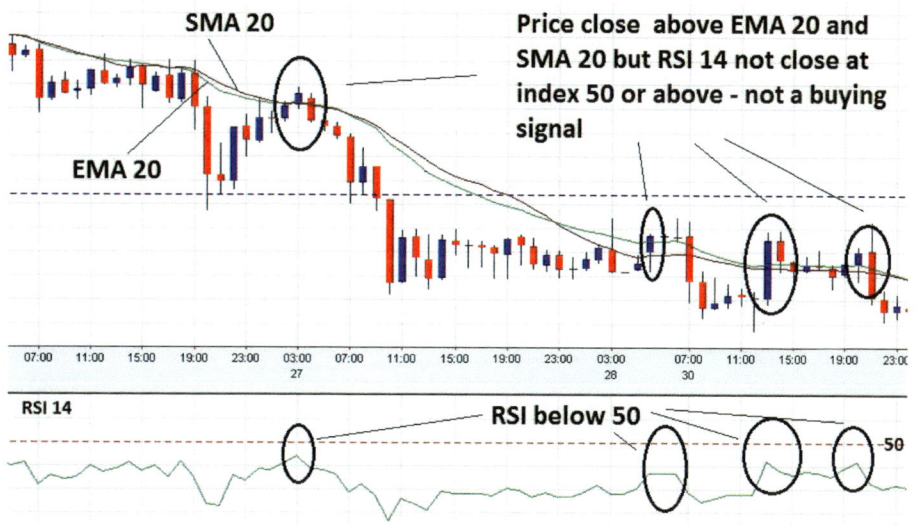

Chart 7: False buying signal

Can you identify opportunity and false signal in chart 8?

Chart 8: opportunity and false signal

There are selling, buying and false signal in chart 8, and the details are explained in chart 9.

Focus should be on closing price first then EMA 20 and SMA 20 line position, after that get confirmation from RSI 14

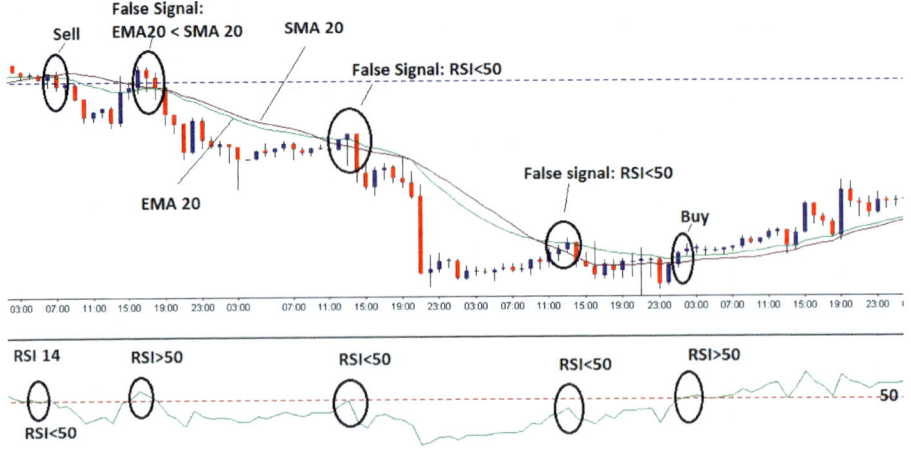

Chart 9: Opportunity and false signal

Combining Trend line, Moving Average and RSI strategy

Looking at each strategy piece by piece seems simple and easy, but when we combine them, it will give a clearer picture to make decision.

Let's look at chart 10, and please identify trading opportunity.

Chart 10: trading opportunity

The identification results are 6 opportunities to start a new position (buy/sell) because they fulfill strategy EMA 20, SMA 20 and RSI 14

Chart 11: opportunities fulfill strategy

What about adding actual trend line in that chart (see chart 12)? Will it change buying and selling decision? The trend line is setup by using non standard SAR (0.02,0)

Chart 12: Adding trend line into chart

By adding trend line, we identify five opportunities to buy/sell (see chart 13). There are two previously identified opportunities not included (red circle) because they are too close to trend line (resistance line), when it is too close to trend line, it is better to wait the price break trend line.

So, not all EMA 20, SMA 20 and RSI 14 buying or selling signal need execution, there must be a consideration on risk and benefit when the price close to trend line. Patience is important in this part.

Chart 13: identifying new opportunities by adding trend line

CHAPTER 4

FORECASTING THE NEXT TARGET

In business, making a forecast needs market trend information. The sales and marketing people will inform company what are the current customers buying trend and competitors price action and after that company make strategy and forecast on its products, inventories, labors, etc. by year, month, week or even day.

In forex trading, making a forecast also needs market trend information; the trend can be seen in market price behavior which is reflected in chart. By using price trend chart, traders are be able to make a forecast on monthly, weekly, day, hourly or minutes target price.

Parabolic SAR (0.02,0) will be used for drawing trend line (support and resistance). Several trend lines around 3-5 (support and resistance) can be drawn from historical chart to make forecasts by minutes, hourly, daily, weekly, or monthly. The price target is actually the next resistance or support line.

Chart 14: Forecasting with real buying execution

Chart 14 shows AUD/USD real example of buying execution when EMA 20 line above SMA 20 line and price close above EMA 20 plus RSI 14 index above 50 at price 0.9364 with 30 pips stop loss, the forecast or target price is around 0,9435 (resistance line), beyond this, the next target is the upper resistance line. If it fails, the down trend target is around 0.9300

We can see the forecast/target result in chart 15 when the price hit up trend target at resistance line. If you noticed that on date 9 (red circle), price below EMA 20 and SMA 20, RSI below index 50, profit can be taken at this level if you are still monitoring the chart.

Chart 15: price hit uptrend target

What about weekly trend for AUD/USD?

Chart 16: weekly forecast chart AUD/USD

We draw the AUD/USD trend line by using Parabolic SAR(0.02,0). Chart 16 shows the nearest resistance as the nearest target is around 0.9800. The target price is always the nearest resistance line and it moves along with the trend line each, so each week we can monitor the nearest resistance price level and change the target price as no one knows when it will touch the resistance line.

In chart 17, we can see the price move which fail to hit the resistance line and it reversed (EMA 20 and SMA 20 cross, RSI<50) to target the support line.

Chart 17: Weekly chart AUD/USD

CHAPTER 5

EXERCISES AND ANSWERS

In this chapter you can do some exercises yourself to find the opportunities or disaster, and then compare them to the answers. Try not to find the answers before trying them first.

Exercise 1:

Please find the opportunities and false trading signal in chart 18?

Chart 18: exercise 1

Answer 1:

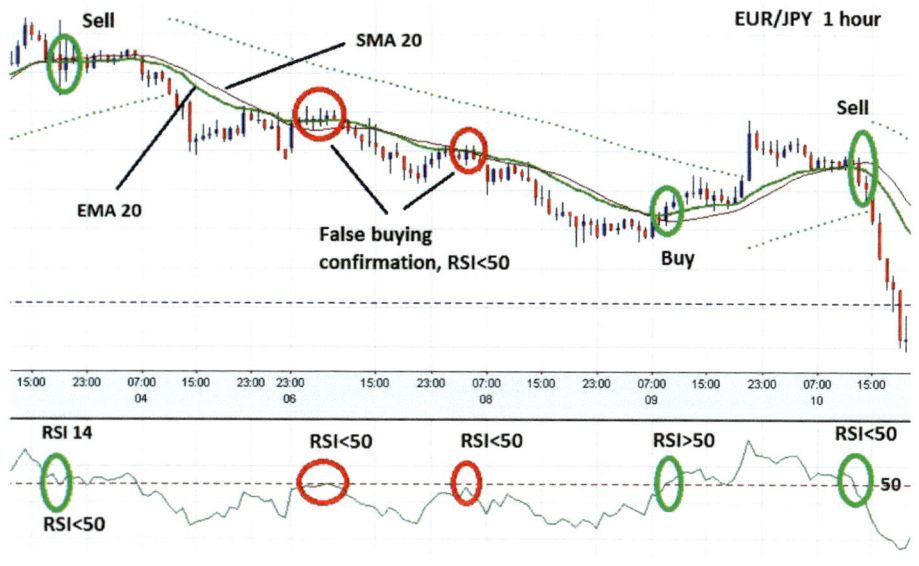

Chart 19: answer 1

In chart 19, after those 2 red circles (point A and B), there are EMA 20 and SMA 20 cross and we do not point that as opportunities with assumption the initial selling position (first green circle) has not been closed and the profit still keep running.

Exercise 2:

Please find your preferred entry point in chart 20?

Chart 20: exercise 2

Answer 2:

Chart 21: answer 2

From chart 21, we can see point A and B as opportunities to trade, both prices close above EMA 20 and SMA 20 with EMA 20 line above SMA 20 line. It is fine to enter at point A or B but there are some considerations: point A risk is higher because the price has run above trend line 2 but unable to close above it, the chance for a reversal is high. Point B risk is lower because the price has closed 2 times in a row above trend line 2 and the chance to hit or even break trend line 1 is higher.

Exercise 3:

Please find the opportunity or disaster if you start from point A and what should we do?

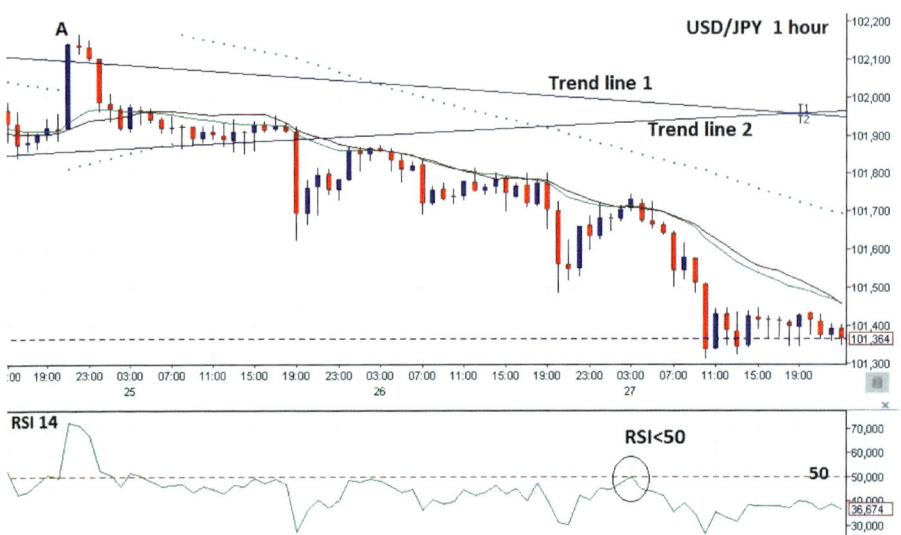

Chart 22: exercise 3

Answer 3:

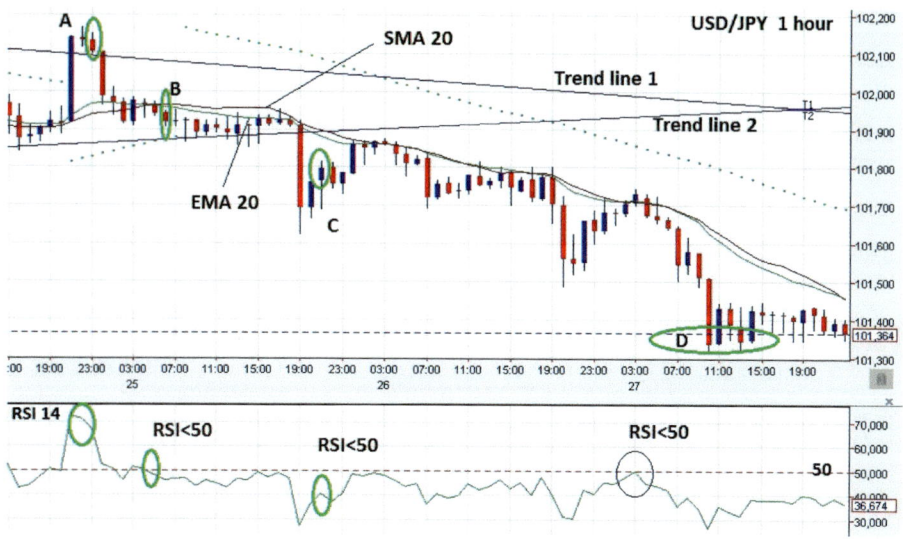

Chart 23: answer 3

At point A, there is an opportunity to buy USD/JPY (green circle) because the price has closed 2 times in a row above trend line 1, but the disaster come, the price keep going down, what should we do? As long as it does not hit stop loss position (i.e.30 pips), we do nothing, but point B is a little bit difficult situation because EMA 20 line below SMA 20 and price below them plus RSI<50, it is a selling confirmation. At this situation we cut the loss first but we do not execute selling position because the price is too close to trend line 2 (if trend line 2 is far enough, it is a good idea to start a selling position), and waiting for another break out. The 2nd break out is at point C and we can execute selling position as the price has closed 2 times in a row below trend line 2, let the profit run until RSI 14>=50 or there is consolidation of price (point D) or use ratio 1:1 i.e. Your stop loss is 30; your profit is also 30 pips.

Exercise 4

At point A, there is buying opportunity after the price close above trend line1, but at point B the price close below trend line 1 several times, are we doing "cut loss" at point B? Why?

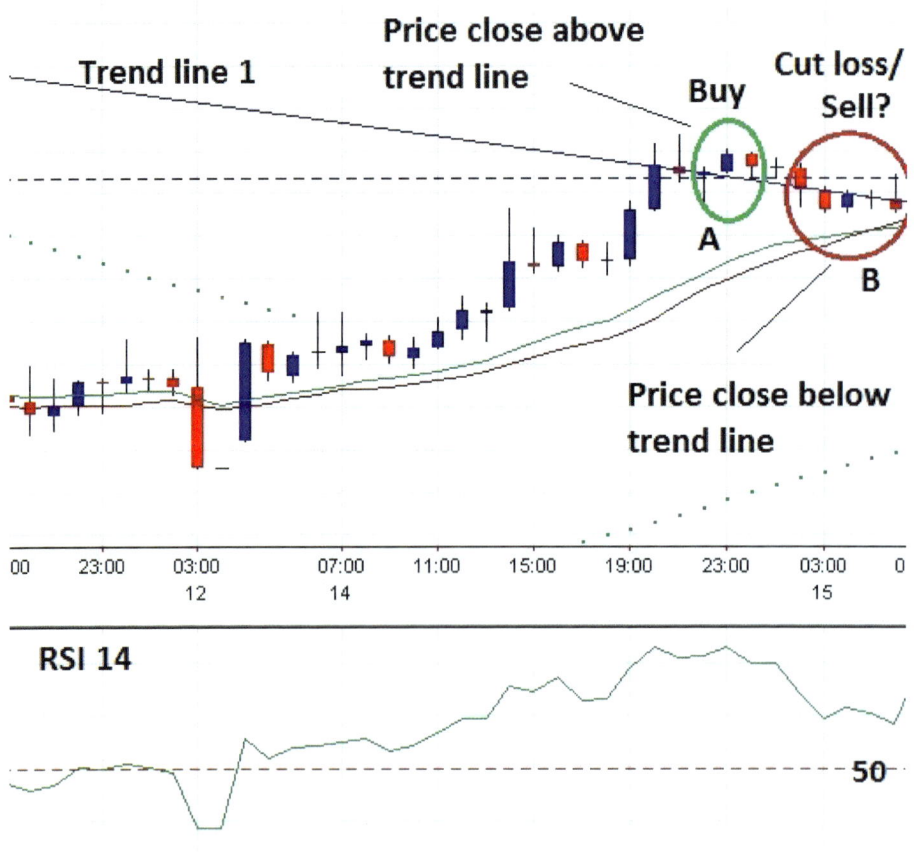

Chart 24: exercise 4

Answer 4:

Chart 25: answer 4

After buying execution at point A, we should not do "cut loss" easily because we have decided the execution with some strong reasons and to cut loss there must be strong reasons to do that. At point B, although the price closes several times below trend line, the closing price is still above EMA 20 and SMA 20 plus RSI still above index 50, so we do nothing at point B.

Exercise 5:

From chart 26, please analyze what activities happened in point A, B, C, D, and E?

Chart 26: exercise 5

Answer 5:

Chart 27: answer 5

Point A: the price close 2 times above trend line and RSI>50, there are reasons to buy at point A, the price go down after buying execution but EMA 20 line still above SMA 20 line so no "cut loss" confirmation.

Point B: The price swing has hit stop loss level and no more position at this point, waits for the next opportunities.

Point C: Buying opportunities as the price close 2 times in a row above the trend line, try to recover the losses first with ratio 1:1 (i.e. stop loss 30 and gain 30 pips) or if the margin balance still at safe level, there is chance to double the position to recover loss and make some gain.

Point D: Selling opportunities as the price close 2 times in a row below trend line. After point D, the price suddenly hit the trend line but we have no choice for this sudden movement, and need to wait whether the second price close above trend line or not for cut loss decision.

Point E: Time to take profit as there is chance for price consolidation. The profit can be also taken with ratio 1:1 and not necessary at point E.

CHAPTER 7

QUESTIONS AND ANSWERS

1. **What should we do during price consolidation period?**

    During consolidation period or side way movement, the price will swing in between support and resistance and we start confusing with the direction. There are two things we can do, first: using trend line strategy, waiting for the price close 2 times in a row above the trend line (support/resistance) to see the winner; second: look at higher time frame i.e. 2, 4, 8 hours or daily time frames to get a bigger view of trend. Sometimes it is not easy to realize that we are in early consolidation period when we execute trading by using EMA 20, SMA 20 and RSI 14, and if we stuck in this period, let the stop loss play its role and then make trading decision later using trend line strategy if stop loss is hit.

2. **Is this book the best trading strategy?**

    There is no best trading strategy guarantees you win in every trade, the point of all trading models are to reduce risk and increase chance to win. This book trading model is derived from daily business activities by using trend and price as main tools, and use technical indicator as supporting confirmation so you know the reason of your execution or losses.

3. **Is this trading model only for 1 hour time frame?**

No, it can be applied to any time frame i.e. 10 minutes, 30 minutes, 2 hours, 8 hours, daily, weekly, etc. However the lower time frame the more volatile the price movement, and the higher time frame, the bigger stop loss margin required.

4. **Are we considering non standard SAR (0.02,0) for buying/selling?**

The non standard SAR (0.02,0) is used for drawing trend line purpose and not used for triggering buying/selling action.

5. **Can we use the non standard SAR (0.02,0) to draw Fibonacci charts?**

The non standard SAR (0.02,0) is the basic concept to draw all Fibonacci charts because we know the correct highest and lowest price.

6. **Which one is better for execution, using trend line strategy" or using EMA 20, SMA 20 AND RSI 14?**

As explained earlier, the main strategy is trend line but sometimes traders want to play in between the support and resistance line or playing with the price swing, however we need to play it safe and fast as the bulls and bears are fighting fiercely between trend lines. Relative Strength Index (RSI) is chosen as supporting tool because it is more sensitive to price.

-    End   -

Printed in Great Britain
by Amazon